The Home Fronts in the Civil War

Dale Anderson

WORLD ALMANAC® LIBRARY

Please visit our web site at: www.worldalmanaclibrary.com
For a free color catalog describing World Almanac® Library's
list of high-quality books and multimedia programs,
call 1-800-848-2928 (USA) or 1-800-387-3178 (Canada).
World Almanac® Library's fax: (414) 332-3567.

Library of Congress Cataloging-in-Publication Data available
upon request from publisher. Fax (414) 336-0157 for the
attention of the Publishing Records Department.

ISBN 0-8368-5587-6 (lib. bdg.)
ISBN 0-8368-5596-5 (softcover)

First published in 2004 by
World Almanac® Library
330 West Olive Street, Suite 100
Milwaukee, WI 53212 USA

Copyright © 2004 by World Almanac® Library.

Produced by Discovery Books
Project editor: Geoff Barker
Editor: Valerie J. Weber
Designer and page production: Laurie Shock, Shock Design, Inc.
Photo researcher: Rachel Tisdale
Consultant: Andrew Frank, Assistant Professor of History, Florida
    Atlantic University
Maps: Stefan Chabluk
World Almanac® editorial direction: Mark Sachner
World Almanac® art direction: Tammy Gruenewald

Photo credits: The Bridgeman Art Library: cover; Library of Congress:
title page, pp. 2, 6, 8, 39; Corbis: pp. 7 (left), 10, 14, 16, 20 (top), 23,
24, 30 (both), 32, 33, 34, 38 (both), 40; Peter Newark's American
Pictures: pp. 7 (right), 9, 12, 13, 19, 20 (bottom), 21, 22, 25, 27, 28, 37,
42 (both), 43; Smithsonian Institute: p. 26.

Printed in the United States of America

1 2 3 4 5 6 7 8 9 08 07 06 05 04

*"To my mother, who got me
Bruce Catton; my brother,
who shared my passion for the
Civil War; and my wife and
sons, who cheerfully put up
with several field trips and
countless anecdotes."*

— DALE ANDERSON

Cover: Jean Leon Jerome Ferris's painting *Their Country's Call*
captures the conflicting emotion felt by men and women as
soldiers went off to war.

Contents

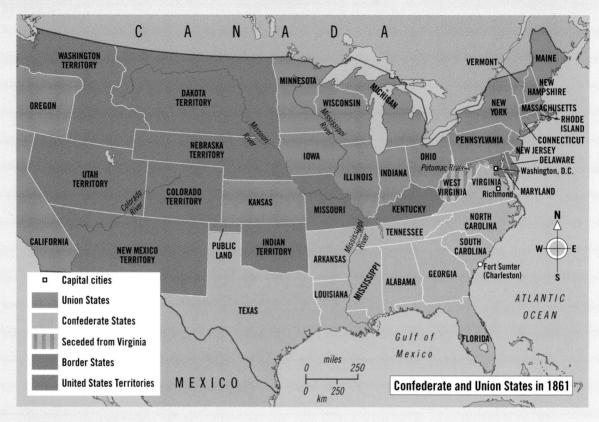

Confederate and Union States in 1861

While the Confederate states covered about as much territory as the Union states, they held fewer people, fewer factories, and fewer railroad tracks and locomotives. These would be significant drawbacks for the Confederacy during the Civil War. The South would also lose part of its support when West Virginia separated from the rest of Virginia in 1863.

The War between the States

The Civil War was fought between 1861 and 1865. It was the bloodiest conflict in United States history, with more soldiers killed and wounded than in any other war. It was also a pivotal event in U.S. history: It transformed the lives of millions of African-American men, women, and children by freeing them from slavery. It also transformed the nation, changing it from a loose confederation of states into a powerful country with a strong central government.

On one side were eleven southern states that had split from the United States to form a new country, the Confederate States of America, led by President Jefferson Davis. They took this step after Abraham Lincoln was elected president of the United

States in 1860. Southerners feared Lincoln would end slavery, which was central to their economy and society. The northern states, or the **Union**, declared this split illegal.

A big question was whether the four **Border States** (Delaware, Maryland, Kentucky, and Missouri) would join the **Confederacy**. They had slavery, too, but they also held many people loyal to the Union. To keep control of these states, Lincoln felt early in the war that he could not risk moving against slavery, fearing that to do so would drive the Border States out of the Union. Later, however, he did declare the emancipation, or freedom, of Southern slaves.

In the Border States, and in many others, families divided sharply, with some men fighting for one side and some for the other. The Civil War has been called a war of "brother against brother."

Fighting broke out on April 12, 1861, when gunners for the South began shelling Union soldiers in Fort Sumter in Charleston Harbor, South Carolina. This attack led Lincoln to call for troops to put down what he called an armed rebellion. Thousands of Northerners flocked to the Union army. Thousands of Southerners joined the Confederate army, determined to win independence for their side.

Soldiers in both the Union and Confederate armies suffered the hardships—and occasional boredom—of life in an army camp. They also fought in huge battles with great bravery and heroism. At times, both sides treated their enemies with honor and respect. At other times, they treated them with cruelty and brutality.

The opposing armies fought in two main areas, or theaters. The eastern theater included Pennsylvania, Virginia, and Maryland; the region near the Confederate capital of Richmond, Virginia; and the Union capital of Washington, D.C. The huge western theater stretched from eastern Kentucky and Tennessee down to the Gulf of Mexico and all the way to New Mexico. By the end of the many bloody battles across these lands, the Union won in 1865, and the states reunited into a single country.

In 1861, many people on both sides believed the war would be short and glorious. By the time of the South's defeat in 1865, however, it had proven long and bloody. The soldiers in the field and their commanders won and lost the battles, of course, but the people at home on both sides were critical to the success of the troops. In addition, they often felt the war's destructive effect on their families, jobs, and homes.

CHAPTER ONE

Life at Home

~

Today, officials notify family members when a soldier or sailor is killed or wounded. During the Civil War, such news came from newspaper casualty lists or, as portrayed here, in letters.

The Personal Side

A few million men served in the armies of the Union and Confederacy. Nearly 680,000 of them died. Over a million more were wounded.

To learn if their loved ones were among those numbers, people scanned the lists of **casualties** in newspapers after a battle for the name of a husband, father, or brother. However, they still could not be sure their close relatives or friends had survived. Casualty lists were not error free, and tens of thousands of soldiers on both sides died not in battle but in a camp or hospital.

This Confederate soldier's jacket contains a letter home and the image of a loved one in a locket.

For many people at home, the bad news arrived in a letter. Soldiers sometimes wrote their parents of a brother's death. Others had to tell life-long friends of a neighbor's passing. These letters could jolt the recipients.

Some people rushed to military hospitals to care for wounded family members. Some, like poet Walt Whitman, were fortunate enough to see the wounded recover. Others simply shared their loved ones' final moments.

News from Home and the Field

Letters did not carry only bad news. Soldiers reported on their lives in

WALT WHITMAN

Born on Long Island, New York, in 1819, Walt Whitman grew up in Brooklyn. He entered journalism and became a newspaper editor. Whitman also began writing poetry, using a new style of unrhymed verse. In 1855, his first book of poetry, Leaves of Grass, *appeared.*

In 1862, Whitman went to a field hospital to care for his wounded brother. He then moved to Washington, D.C., where he got a job as a government clerk and spent his spare time caring for wounded soldiers.

After the war, Whitman brought out many editions of Leaves of Grass. *Many critics thought his poems immoral and objected to how unconventional they were. For these reasons, he never gained great popularity in his time.* Leaves of Grass *sold much better in the years after his death, however, and today, he is considered a master U.S. poet. He died in 1892.*

camp and in battle. Letters from home talked about children and family, crops and farm animals or changes in the city. Both soldiers and family members often wrote about their faith in God, and letters often expressed hope that the war would end soon—and safely. As Union soldier Lucius Mox wrote his wife in 1865, "I am sure they will be the happiest days of my life when I get out of this miserable camp and tiresome service."

Women at Home

Until the men made it home, women had to shoulder extra burdens. More than 10 percent of the men of both sides served in the armed forces during the Civil War. If just men from their late teens to early forties are counted, the figures rise to 50 percent or more in many states.

"Dead! Dead! Dead! O my brothers! What have we lived for except you? We, who would have so gladly laid down our lives for yours, are left desolate to mourn over all we loved and hoped for."

Southerner Sarah Morgan
in her diary, 1865

Soldiers sent home letters detailing camp life and the fierce action they saw in battles. Some, like the Union soldier who wrote this letter, included drawings.

When these men left for war, women had to do much of their labor. Farmwomen added planting, weeding, and harvesting crops to their usual jobs of vegetable gardening, cooking, cleaning, sewing, and child rearing. The wives of shopkeepers tended to family stores, while other women worked in factories.

Women played important political as well as economic roles, helping spur many men to enlist, sometimes by shaming them. Southern nurse Kate Cumming wrote in her journal early in the war—and doubtlessly communicated to many men in person—the idea that a "man did not deserve the name of man if he did not fight for his country." Women also banded together to make socks and blankets, bandages and food. Thousands on both sides became nurses.

HARPER'S WEEKLY
A JOURNAL OF CIVILIZATION.

Vol. V.—No. 238.]   NEW YORK, SATURDAY, JULY 20, 1861.   [SINGLE COPIES SIX CENTS.
[$2.50 PER YEAR IN ADVANCE.

Entered according to Act of Congress, in the Year 1861, by Harper & Brothers, in the Clerk's Office of the District Court for the Southern District of New York.

As this Winslow Homer engraving for *Harper's Weekly* shows, many women left their homes to work in factories during the Civil War.

Many women were lonely during the war. Some moved in with their parents or sisters simply to have company. One woman wrote that "numerous ladies . . . are reduced to marry men whom they do not love merely because they crave affection."

When the Armies Came

At times, the war came frightfully near the home fronts, especially in the South, where the Union army advanced into large areas over the course of the war. In the North, which saw few invasions, only a few areas saw similar destruction.

Panicked citizens fled Savannah, Georgia, when Union forces occupied nearby Tybee Island in late 1861.

Some areas suffered greatly, such as Virginia, which was often the site of fierce battles. Officers seized homes to use as headquarters or hospitals, burning furniture in campfires. Soldiers digging trenches destroyed fields. Felling of trees for barricades leveled forests. Even the mere passing of an army was destructive—soldiers took families' food and animals. Officers might leave behind papers promising payment, but the owners could not always collect.

Several Southern cities suffered terrible fires, which were actually the work of both sides. Retreating Confederate soldiers burned cotton and food and other army supplies so they would not fall into Union hands. Union soldiers either added to the destruction or did little to stop it.

> *"First bursts of smoke, dense, black volumes, then tongues of flame, then huge waves of fire roll up into the sky: Presently the skeletons of great warehouses stand out in relief against . . . sheets of roaring, blazing, furious flames . . . as one fire sinks, another rises . . . lurid, angry, dreadful to look on."*
>
> Union major Henry Hitchcock in 1927, describing the fire in Atlanta in 1864

Life in the South

~

CHAPTER TWO

*"Our battle against
want and starvation is greater
than against our enemies."*

Confederate government
report, 1863

Hardships and Adjustments

For Confederate civilians, life during the war was very difficult. The Southern states lacked factories so they could not produce everything their people needed. Because Union ships **blockaded** Confederate ports, it was not easy to bring goods in from other countries, either. As a result, prices rose sharply through-out the Civil War.

Factories were set up to make items that had not been manufactured in the South before, and people turned to making things like soap, candles, clothing, and shoes at home. Sometimes, they had to be creative with unusual materials, turning palm-tree leaves into hats and grinding okra seeds instead of coffee beans.

As Union armies moved into the South, many Southerners abandoned their homes, sometimes moving several times. Some people joined relatives in another town, and many moved to cities. As more and more people gathered, however, food shortages—especially of sugar, coffee, meat, and fresh produce—arose in cities. One of the worst shortages was salt. In an age before refrigeration, this simple product was needed to preserve meat.

Food shortages had several causes. First, much of the South had been plant-ed in cotton before the war, and people were slow to shift to growing food. Second, as the Union conquered more territory, less farmland became available for grow-ing crops in the Confederacy. Finally, the Southern transportation network could not always move food to the cities.

Some wealthy Southerners continued to live well, at least for a while. Ships that ran the Union blockades typically brought in luxury goods such as silk and wine because selling them brought the ships' owners the best profits.

Food Shortages and Riots

Shortages sometimes led to unrest. On April 2, 1863, a riot erupted in

Richmond's bread riot was not the only outbreak of civil unrest in the South. On the whole, however, Southerners put up with four years of death, destruction, and hardship with resilience.

Richmond when a group of women marched to the home of Virginia's governor to demand more food and lower prices. He listened sympathetically but offered no solutions. The crowd, now angry, moved to a nearby shopping area and began breaking into stores and looting goods. Troops arrived, and the two groups—angry citizens and nervous soldiers—faced one another. President Jefferson Davis appeared and emptied his pockets of all his money, flinging it to the crowd. Then he warned them to disperse or he would order the soldiers to fire. The people went home.

In other cities threatened by riots, local governments moved to ease the situation by supplying the very poor with food and other necessities. They could never end the shortages, however; hunger gnawed at the Confederates throughout the long war.

Southerners mounted charity efforts to help the poor, especially the families of soldiers. People donated what they could, but sometimes the strains were simply too much. One Southern wife wrote her husband a painful letter. "Since your connection with the Confederate army I have been prouder of you than ever before. . . . But before God, Edward, unless you come home, we must die." Her husband left the army to come home,

The South depended on the hard work of black slaves. Thousands of them escaped slavery by walking to safety with Union armies—where they were happy to lend their energy to the war effort.

but he was caught. Returned to his unit, he was later killed in battle.

Southerners' Worries

Civil unrest was not Southerners' only worry. Many Southern whites feared that enslaved African Americans would rise up in rebellion.

This fear was the basis for an **exemption** from the **draft** law that passed in late 1862. The exemption allowed men who owned twenty or more slaves to avoid serving in the army. White Southerners feared that white women, left alone on a large plantation, would not be able to control the African-American slaves. As the war continued, however, white Southerners found that slave rebellions did not occur, and their fears lessened.

The other major worry, of course, was what the advancing Union soldiers would do. Many people in the South

"Is it possible that Congress thinks . . . our women can control the slaves and oversee the farms? Do they suppose that our patriotic mothers, sisters and daughters can assume and discharge the active duties . . . of an overseer? Certainly not. They know better."

Macon Daily Telegraph, 1862

"Bummers," an organized band of Union foragers who gathered food for General William Sherman's troops, raid a Southerner's farm in about 1864.

thought that the Union soldiers were barbarians who would loot homes and hurt women. At times, those fears were realized—invading armies sometimes treated civilians brutally and ruthlessly. They stole anything of value, ran off with farm animals, and burned homes.

The reality of invasion was not always so bad, however. Obviously,

Union soldiers did not destroy all Southern homes. Still, there was often friction between Southern women and Northern soldiers. A reporter for the *New York World* newspaper said that Confederate women spoke with "vengeance and venom I have never seen exceeded." Many Southern women both hated and feared these soldiers.

WHY THE CONFEDERACY FAILED

Southerners began the war with high hopes. Many were confident that their armies would defeat Northerners, who they thought were weak and cowardly. So why did the Southerners lose the war?

There are many reasons, including the fact that the South was outnumbered and out-gunned. The North had more money, more men, more resources, and more railroads to move those men and resources. Shortages of food and supplies plagued Southern armies, making it difficult for them to keep up the fight. While Confederate armies fought bravely and many rebel generals led well, battle losses whittled down the South's military power—its men could not be replaced. At the same time, the North was able to obtain fresh troops to the end. After the war, many Southerners explained the outcome simply in those terms. However, many more factors were at work in the Union victory.

Northern power could be applied over a long war only if the Union had the will to fight. President Abraham Lincoln never lost that will, and he kept Northerners focused on the war.

The Union also won key turning points. Its September 1862 victory at Antietam (also known as Sharpsburg) defeated the first great Confederate invasion. Equally important, it gave Lincoln an occasion to issue the Emancipation Proclamation, which freed slaves in Confederate states. Great Britain and France would have been happy to see the United States weakened by being divided, but they were unwilling to back the Confederacy if it did not seem to have a chance to win the war. They were also unwilling to support the Confederacy once the Union made the war not just a fight for reunion but a crusade against slavery. The Union win at Gettysburg, Pennsylvania, in July 1863 turned back Lee's second invasion of the North and left his army too weak to ever invade the North again.

The war's outcome was still in doubt in the summer of 1864. By that time, many in the North were weary of the conflict and hoped for peace. If Lincoln had not won reelection, General George McClellan, a Democrat, would have become president and might have accepted the Confederates' terms for peace. That summer, however, the Union army captured Atlanta, and Northern spirits revived. Lincoln was reelected, and the war continued.

"What General [Robert E.] Lee surrendered was the skeleton, the mere ghost of the [army], which had been gradually worn down by the combined agencies of numbers, steam power, railroads, mechanism, and all the resources of physical sciences."

Confederate general Jubal Early, analyzing why the South lost, 1872

CHAPTER THREE

Life in the North

~

The Union army used trains to move troops and supplies. The demand for locomotives like this one meant profits for manufacturers and railroad companies.

The Economy of the North

As the Southern states **seceded** between December 1860 and May 1861, the North's economy went into a slump. Business owners worried about the effect of the Union's breakup, and workers left their jobs to enter the army.

Eventually, however, the economy recovered, and many industries boomed. Railroads grew at a rapid pace. Companies that supplied uniforms, weapons, ammunition, and food to the army had plenty of orders. The textile industry, the nation's largest at the time, suffered at first from the lack of cotton. As Union armies gained control of Southern territory, however, cotton once more came north and the mills rebounded.

Northerners faced rising prices, though increases were not as sharp as for Southerners. The steeper prices hurt factory workers in particular, because their wages did not go up to match the increasing cost of necessities such as food. Many workers organized unions to try to win better wages and working conditions, though these efforts seldom worked. The army was often called in to put down **strikes**, especially by workers in industries that supplied goods for the war such as uniforms, railway equipment, and weapons.

Paying for the War

To finance the war, the Union government needed huge sums of money. By the war's end, it had spent more than $3 billion. Nearly $2.7 billion of that money came from borrowing.

The government also raised $667 million in taxes. One source of tax revenue was an income tax. Even more revenue came from the excise tax created in 1862, which taxed goods like alcohol and tobacco; raw materials such as wood, cloth, and leather; manufactured goods; and even people's occupations.

THE TIDE OF IMMIGRANTS

In general, the Northern economy grew during the war, which was one reason why people kept immigrating to the United States. Immigration dropped slightly at the beginning of the war. By 1863, however, more people were coming to the United States than before the war.

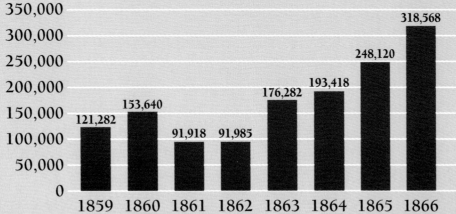

Immigration to the United States, 1859–1866

Year	Immigrants
1859	121,282
1860	153,640
1861	91,918
1862	91,985
1863	176,282
1864	193,418
1865	248,120
1866	318,568

The U.S. government met the need for money in another way—by printing it. Before the war, money took the form of gold or silver coins or paper money that could be exchanged for gold. Late in 1861, however, the government had too little gold to meet the possible demand for it. It temporarily halted its promise to trade paper notes for gold. Soon after, Congress allowed the government to print paper money that was not backed by gold. During the war, the government printed more than $400 million in these paper "greenbacks."

The growth in government spending led to corruption. Some business people—and some army officers—took advantage of the situation to make fortunes. This was a particular problem in the parts of the South that Union armies occupied. There, Northerners could make fortunes by buying Southern cotton and selling it for ten times more in the North. Ironically, this trade also helped keep Southern armies in the field. In late 1862, one Southern army sold cotton to Northerners and used the money it earned to buy supplies it needed.

Violence Erupts— People Help

Crime increased somewhat, particularly in the cities, during the war years. In many areas, the proportion of women in prison was higher during the war than before. In New York City, the number of children who were arrested rose sharply. The reasons for this are unclear. Perhaps the absence of working husbands and fathers pushed women and children into crime, or maybe women and children drew more police attention.

There were occasional outbreaks of mob violence in the North as well as the South. Mobs attacked newspaper offices for political reasons, and some chased out people suspected of Southern sympathies. The most extreme outbreak of mob violence was the New York draft riot of 1863. Poor workers, many of them Irish immigrants, worried that if they were drafted, freed African Americans would get their jobs because, at that time, employers could pay lower wages to blacks. When Union draft officers came to the city in mid-July, the workers' anger erupted into a riot. Over several days, rioters burned buildings and attacked blacks. More than one hundred people were killed in the riot. Nearly 10 percent were African American, but the great majority were rioters shot by soldiers brought in to quell the uprising.

While crime and unrest increased during the war, so did many positive movements. In the North, as in the South, many people worked to help

New York City saw three days of chaos during the draft riots of 1863. The people rioting against the draft did not sympathize with the South. They were lashing out against what they saw as the threat of freed slaves willing to work for lower wages.

the poor, sick, and wounded. People also raised money to help soldiers' families, and the U.S. Sanitary Commission improved medical care for wounded soldiers.

Federal Changes

Some U.S. symbols that are now well known had their beginnings during the conflict. In November of 1863, Lincoln made Thanksgiving a national holiday. The next year, the words "In God We Trust" appeared on U.S. coins for the first time. Congress also created the Congressional Medal of Honor for soldiers during the war.

While some states left the Union, others joined it. West Virginia split from Virginia, and the U.S. Congress allowed it to join the Union in 1863. Nevada became a state the following year. New territorial governments were organized in Arizona, Idaho, and Montana.

Before the Civil War, the U.S. Capitol still did not have the dome that tops its central section today. The dome was built during the war and completed in 1863.

Two laws paved the way for millions of people to move onto the Great Plains. In 1862, Congress passed the Homestead Act, which allowed anyone to claim 160 acres (65 hectares) of public land and gain ownership of it just by staying on it for five years. Over the next twenty years, about 500,000 people built farms under this law. Later that year, Congress passed the Pacific Railroad Act, which opened the way for companies to build a railroad stretching from the Mississippi River to the Pacific Ocean.

In July of 1862, Congress passed the Morrill Act. Under this law, each state received 30,000 acres (12,150 ha) of public land for each representative that it sent to Congress. The land could be used by the state or sold, with the proceeds used to set up public colleges and universities. This law led to the creation of many colleges.

Mary Walker, one of the few women trained as a doctor before the war, won the Congressional Medal of Honor for her work tending the wounded. She was the only woman awarded the Medal of Honor during the war.

Homesteaders pose at the log home they built in Kansas. The Homestead Act gave thousands of settlers land at low prices—at the expense of the Native Americans who had lived on the land until whites seized it.

MAKING WEST VIRGINIA

West Virginia was once part of Virginia. The soil and climate of this mountainous area were not suitable for plantation agriculture so few slaves lived there. When Virginia seceded, many people in this western part wanted to separate so they could return to the Union. Under the **Constitution**, *however, a state legislature had to agree to split an existing state in two. The eastern, pro-Confederate forces dominated the state legislature, and they would not grant the western counties the right to leave.*

Western Virginia leaders found a way around the law, however, setting up a new state government loyal to the Union. Then this unofficial state legislature voted to allow the counties to leave the state. In October 1861, voters in the area approved the move. In June 1863, the state formally entered the Union.

CHAPTER FOUR

African Americans in the War

*"[Slaveholders] tried to take
their Negroes with them but they would
not go. They shot down their Negroes in many
instances because they would not go with them. They
tied them behind their wagons, and tried to drag them
off; but the Negroes would not go. The majority of
Negroes remained behind and came into our lines."*

Union general Rufus Saxton, 1861

Moving to Freedom

The Civil War raised Southern African Americans' hopes that slavery would end. Many acted on that hope, leaving their homes and plantations and making their way toward Union armies. The exact number of slaves who freed themselves in this way cannot be known, but estimates run as high as 500,000.

White Southerners feared that the war would become a social revolution and African-American slaves would revolt or run away in massive numbers. Thousands of slaves did escape to freedom. White Southerners tried to hunt them down, sometimes using dogs, before they could reach Union lines.

A group of "contrabands" (the name given to former slaves by Union brigadier general Ben Butler) took a break in their work on behalf of the Union army to pose for this picture.

Early in the war, Union commanders wondered how these slaves should be treated. The answer came in spring of 1861. Three blacks had fled to Brigadier General Ben Butler's army in eastern Virginia. A Southerner came to Butler's army to bring them back, but Butler refused to let them go, calling them "contrabands of war." Contraband is property of an enemy that an army seizes. News of Butler's action traveled quickly, and more slaves came into his camp. Within two months, there were nearly a thousand.

Across the South, other Union commanders treated the former slaves as Butler had done. They named officers to see to the needs of the "contrabands" and made sure that they received food, clothing, shelter, and medical care.

The government also tried to help these blacks earn a living. The army hired many to do work in the camps, and some were put to work on plantations that had been seized. Many worked harder and with greater pleasure than they had ever done under slavery.

The government and army efforts were somewhat disorganized. On March 3, 1865, however, late in

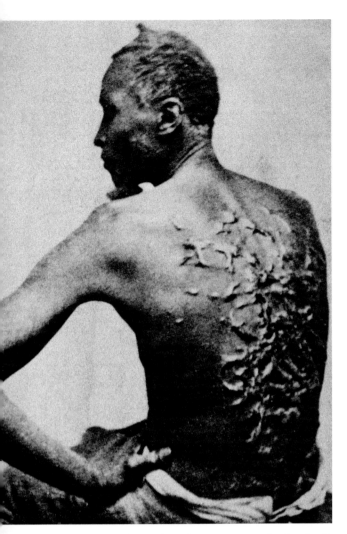

The reminders of a whipping scar the back of this African American, highlighting the brutal side of slavery. This particular man joined the Union army, where he became a corporal.

the war, Congress passed a law creating the Freedmen's Bureau, an agency to help blacks adjust to their new lives as free people.

Emancipation Becomes Policy

The larger issue of what to do about slavery remained unanswered, however.

President Lincoln had taken office vowing that he intended not to undo slavery but only to limit its spread to the territories. This stand was based on his belief that the federal government did not have the power to make such changes. It was also based on a political reality—his need to keep the Border States in the Union. Lincoln

Lincoln's Emancipation Proclamation was, in a sense, a half-measure. It freed none of the slaves in Union-controlled territory but only those in land controlled by the Confederacy. Still, it clearly made the end of slavery a goal of the war.

feared that if he abolished slavery, they would join the South.

Meanwhile, Lincoln and Congress took some steps to end slavery. In April 1862, Congress approved Lincoln's plan to offer money to any state that passed a law ending slavery; it also freed slaves in the District of Columbia. Two months later, Congress ended slavery in the territories. In July, it declared that any Southern blacks who made their way to the Union Army were free. That month, Lincoln decided to free all slaves in the South, although he did not issue the Emancipation Proclamation until September of 1862. The final version came out early in 1863.

War Effort

Blacks played many different roles in the Civil War. Many Northern blacks pushed hard to make the end of slavery a goal of the war, a cause for which Frederick Douglass had long fought. Early in the Civil War, he issued several calls for freedom for blacks, which were answered when Lincoln finally issued the Emancipation Proclamation.

Many African Americans had volunteered to fight as soon as the Civil War broke out, but the government refused to accept them. In mid-1862, however, the government switched its policy: Congress passed a law that allowed blacks in the army, although the soldiers would have to fight in all-black units. By the end of the war, about 200,000 African Americans, including Northern blacks and former slaves, had served in the Union army. Even those who did not join the army helped the war effort. Some blacks stayed with the Union armies, working as blacksmiths and carpenters, loading and unloading cargo, and doing other tasks. Some served as spies and scouts in areas they knew or helped Union soldiers who were escaping from Confederate prisons.

Some Northern blacks also established "freedmen's aid societies" in order to raise money to help former slaves with clothing and other goods. Some sent free Northern blacks to Southern areas under Union control, where they established schools and taught freed slaves to read and write.

"To fight against slaveholders, without fighting against slavery, is but a half-hearted business. . . . War for the destruction of liberty must be met with war for the destruction of slavery."

Frederick Douglass, an abolitionist and former African-American slave, 1861

Frederick Douglass, who escaped from slavery before the war, was a powerful voice in favor of having black Union soldiers. Two of his sons were among the more than 200,000 blacks who joined the army.

African-American troops overcame the doubts of many Northern whites and proved themselves in combat.

"Still [hidden] in the woods, the women coming to us twice during the day to bring us food and inform us that a guide will be ready at dark. God bless the poor slaves. At dark Frank took us. . . . [We] traveled all night, making about twenty-two miles."

Lieutenant Hannibal Johnson in 1903, a Union officer who escaped from a Confederate prison camp

"My heart sings a song of thanksgiving, at the thought that even I am permitted to do something for a long-abused race, and aid in promoting a higher, holier, and happier life on the Sea Islands."

Charlotte Forten, a black Northerner who went South to teach freed slaves, 1864

Northern African Americans also made some advances toward more equal rights at home. All states except Indiana eliminated laws giving blacks fewer rights than whites. Indiana finally dropped its law in 1866. In Washington, D.C., the U.S. Congress passed a federal law that allowed African Americans to testify in trials, a right they had never enjoyed before. In Philadelphia, Pennsylvania, blacks mounted a long campaign to end **segregation** on the city's streetcars. In 1867, the Pennsylvania legislature passed a law that ended segregation in the whole state. Still, Northern African Americans suffered unfair and unequal treatment throughout the war. They would not gain their full rights until more than a hundred years after the Civil War ended.

CHAPTER FIVE

Creating a New Nation

"The man and the hour have met!" cheered one Southern politician as he introduced the Confederacy's new president, Jefferson Davis, to a crowd in Montgomery, Alabama. Two days later, Davis was officially sworn into office, a scene shown in this illustration.

The Confederate Constitution

In early February 1861, Southern leaders met in Montgomery, Alabama, to create a new national government and constitution and to enact policies that would lead a nation to war. Their actions would affect the lives of the men and women who experienced the war firsthand and entire civilian populations. These leaders came from South Carolina, Georgia, Florida, Alabama, Mississippi, and Louisiana—the states that had seceded by this time. Later, Virginia, North Carolina, Tennessee, Arkansas, and Texas joined the Confederacy.

These Confederate delegates produced a new constitution. Like the original U.S. Constitution, it set up three branches of government. The executive branch, including the president and vice president, carried out the laws. The legislative branch—a Congress with a House and a Senate—made the laws. A Supreme Court headed the judicial branch.

The Confederate Constitution differed in key ways from its model, however. The U.S. Constitution opens by declaring that "We the people" are creating a government. The Confederate Constitution stated that the people were acting through the states, which kept certain rights. "Each State," it said, was "acting in its **sovereign** and independent character." This wording put into practice the Southern theory of states' rights. This political idea held that the nation was formed of individual states, that those states had more power than the national government over some issues, and that the states could enter or leave the nation at any time.

DIFFERENCE BETWEEN CONFEDERATE AND U.S. CONSTITUTIONS

Topic	Confederate	United States
Presidential term	Six years; cannot be reelected	Four years; can be reelected
Presidential veto power	President can veto individual items in a spending bill	President can only veto an entire bill
Cabinet officers' roles	Can have seats in Congress	Do not have seats in Congress
Spending bills	Two-thirds majority in both houses needed to pass any spending item not requested by the president	Simple majority in both houses needed to pass any spending item
General powers of Congress	Does not have the "elastic clause," denying Congress the right to pass any law needed for the public welfare	Does have the "elastic clause," giving Congress the right to pass any law needed for the public welfare
Taxing powers of Congress	Cannot tax imports or exports	Can tax imports and exports
Slavery	No law banning slavery allowed; slavery guaranteed in territories	Congress could act against slavery; slavery not guaranteed in territories
Amendments	Can only be proposed by states: only two-thirds of states needed	Can be proposed by Congress or by states; three-quarter of states needed

JUDAH BENJAMIN

Born in Saint Croix in the Caribbean in 1811, Judah Benjamin came with his family to the United States as a child. They settled in Charleston, South Carolina, where Benjamin was educated. He studied law and moved to New Orleans, where he became a highly successful lawyer. In 1852, he became the first Jew elected to the U.S. Senate, speaking skillfully on behalf of Southern interests.

Benjamin served as the Confederacy's first attorney general and then, briefly, as secretary of war. He came under heavy criticism in this post—some of it based on mistrust because he was Jewish—although he was only carrying out Davis's orders. Out of loyalty, Benjamin took the blame and resigned. Davis rewarded him by naming him secretary of state. After the war, Benjamin settled in England, where he once again practiced law. He died in 1884.

The Confederate Government

The delegates in Montgomery also selected a president, Jefferson Davis of Mississippi. His vice president was Alexander Stephens of Georgia.

Davis named a cabinet, the officials to lead each department in the executive branch. They were under constant criticism throughout the war. Only two, Secretary of the Navy Stephen R. Mallory and Postmaster General John H. Reagan, stayed in

The Confederacy issued millions of dollars in paper money. Its value fell steadily throughout the war.

their original posts for the entire war. Judah Benjamin began as attorney general and ended up as secretary of state. Five different men led the war department; none were effective, but that was not entirely their fault. Davis had graduated from the U.S. Military Academy and had headed the U.S. War Department in the 1850s—he wanted to be his own secretary of war.

Challenges for the South

Besides organizing and launching a new government, the Confederacy had to figure out how to finance the war. Treasury Secretary C. G. Memminger began by selling **bonds**, borrowing the money with the promise to repay it later with added interest. Though some bonds were sold, the amount raised was not enough to support the war effort.

The government also financed the war by printing Confederate dollars. At this time, a nation's money only had value if it could be redeemed for its stated worth in gold. Over time, the South used its gold to buy arms and supplies from foreign countries, so less gold was available to back the paper money. When the government printed even more bills, the value of that money dropped further.

"Our Congress is so demoralized, so confused, so depressed."

Mary Chesnut in her diary (1864)

*"You have allowed your **antipathy** to Davis to mislead your judgment. . . . You are wrong because the whole movement originated in a mad purpose to make war on Davis & Company. You are wrong because the movement is joyous to the enemy."*

Senator Herschel Johnson of Georgia in a letter to Alexander Stephens, 1864

In early 1863, the Confederate Congress turned to taxing farm and forest products, property, and income. The government did not have the resources to collect the taxes; in the end, the South never had enough money to fully meet its military needs.

Cotton Policy

The South could have raised money by selling cotton. Southern leaders, however, hoped to stop the flow of cotton to Britain and France and thus shut down the **textile mills** there. They hoped this would force factory owners and workers to pressure their governments to recognize the South as an independent nation.

This strategy failed completely. The cotton crops of the years just before the war had been plentiful; when the war began, overseas factories had an ample supply on hand. Later, factory owners bought cotton from India. Because there was no shortage, there was no political pressure on the British and French governments;

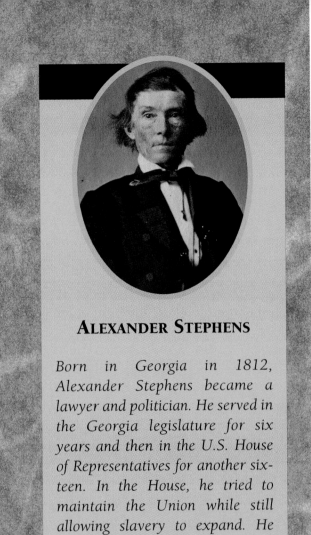

ALEXANDER STEPHENS

Born in Georgia in 1812, Alexander Stephens became a lawyer and politician. He served in the Georgia legislature for six years and then in the U.S. House of Representatives for another sixteen. In the House, he tried to maintain the Union while still allowing slavery to expand. He was against secession, but when Georgia seceded, he joined the Confederacy and helped craft its constitution.

After the war, Stephens was held under arrest for some months. He was later elected to the U.S. House of Representatives and then elected governor of Georgia. He died while governor in 1884.

Dealing with Dissent

Over the years, Jefferson Davis faced much criticism and opposition. At times, he took strong action to stop dissent and restore order. An 1862 law gave him the power to suspend **habeas corpus.** By setting this right aside, the government was able to hold a person under arrest without even charging him or her with a crime. Davis used this power from time to time to call for **martial law** in some areas.

Davis, like most Southerners, believed in states' rights but also thought that during a war, the national government should have more power than the states. Many other Southern leaders disagreed strongly. Members of Congress, state governors, and even Vice President Alexander Stephens often acted to block Davis's attempts to exercise that power. Some governors refused to supply troops in the numbers that Davis requested. An early tax law called on the states to tax people and forward the money to the Confederate government, but most states simply borrowed the money.

Peace Movements

At different times, the governors of Georgia and North Carolina suggested negotiating a separate peace with the Union. In early 1865, President Davis gave in to Vice President Stephens's pressure for a peace settle-

as a result, they did not recognize the South. Meanwhile, cotton rotted in Southern warehouses.

Richmond, like many other Southern cities, erupted in flames when evacuated by Southern forces. The Confederates typically set fire to supplies they could not carry with them.

ment and sent him and two others to meet with President Lincoln and his secretary of state, William Seward. The peace conference was doomed from the start. Stephens and his colleagues insisted on independence for the South, while Lincoln would accept nothing but reunion and the end of slavery.

Davis was not surprised. He had hoped, however, to use the failed peace talks to rally Southerners to a final victory.

By then, it was too late. Within about two months, the disintegrating Southern army became powerless to protect Richmond, Virginia, any longer. As Union troops neared the Confederate capital, the government was forced to flee the city. Soon after, the Southern armies surrendered, and the war was over.

CHAPTER SIX

Lincoln in Office

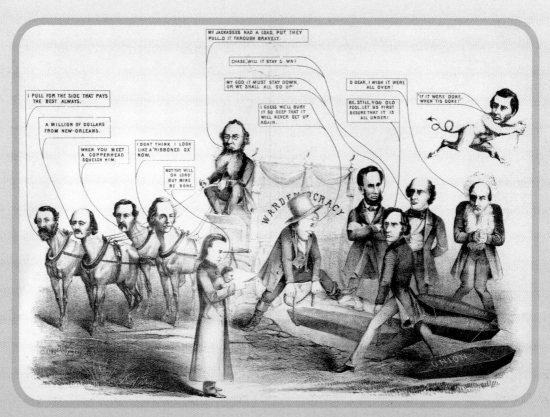

This Northern political cartoon makes clear that Abraham Lincoln faced stiff opposition to his manner of carrying out the war. Here, he and members of his administration are shown burying the Constitution, the Union, and free speech as the cartoonist charges Lincoln with taking away people's basic **civil rights**.

Lincoln and His Cabinet

While Jefferson Davis struggled with opposition in the South, Abraham Lincoln had problems of his own, sometimes with his cabinet. Lincoln, unlike Davis, named several strong Northern leaders to his cabinet. In fact, four members of his cabinet had competed with him to win the nomination of the Republican party for president. Lincoln named these people because he felt that they would have to support him if they were in the cabinet. If left outside the cabinet, they could become rallying points for people who opposed his policies.

"Somebody has plundered the public treasury in a single year as much as the entire yearly [spending] of the [previous administration]."

Representative Henry Dawes, on corruption in the War Department, 1862

Secretary of State William Seward was the first to cause difficulties. Soon after Lincoln took office, Seward wrote him a letter suggesting some foreign policy positions. He also told Lincoln that the government needed a strong person to lead it through the dangerous war. He hinted that he did not think Lincoln capable of doing that work—and that he would be happy to take on the task. Lincoln politely but firmly made it clear that he was the one in charge, and Seward served as a loyal and effective advisor for the rest of the war.

The next problem was Secretary of War Simon Cameron. He was corrupt, giving fat government contracts to friends and allies. Many of the goods his department bought for the army were of poor quality. When Congress began investigating these actions, Lincoln got Cameron to resign. In his place, Lincoln named the incorruptible Edwin Stanton, who ran the War Department efficiently for the rest of the Civil War.

The last Cabinet member to give Lincoln problems was Treasury Secretary Salmon Chase. Late in 1862, Chase tried to force Seward out of the Cabinet. Firmly opposed to slavery, Secretary Chase felt that Seward was convincing Lincoln not to

Salmon Chase, who had run against Lincoln for the Republican nomination for president in 1860, was an effective secretary of the treasury but gave Lincoln frequent political troubles as he pursued his own ambitions.

declare an end to slavery. Lincoln cleverly stopped Chase's move and managed to keep both him and Seward in his Cabinet. Chase, however, remained unhappy with the way Lincoln ran the war. Showing no loyalty to his president, Chase began to try and grab the Republican nomination for president away from Lincoln in 1864. When his efforts failed, he offered to resign from the Cabinet, and Lincoln accepted. Two months later, however, Lincoln named the former treasury secretary as Chief Justice of the Supreme Court, revealing his ongoing respect for Chase.

"I think a man of different qualities from those the President has will be needed for the next four years."

Secretary of the Treasury
Salmon P. Chase, 1864

Lincoln and the Radical Republicans

President Lincoln also had his problems with Congress. Very early in the war, a core group of fellow Republicans became the most powerful members of Congress. Called the "Radical Republicans," they were fiercely opposed to slavery and wanted policies to punish the South

"Free every slave— slay every traitor—burn every rebel mansion, if . . . necessary."

Thaddeus Stevens, speech in the House of Representatives, 1861

during and after the war. The Radicals included Senators Benjamin Wade of Ohio and Zachariah Chandler of Michigan and Pennsylvania Representative Thaddeus Stevens.

Early in the war, the Radicals tried to push Lincoln to end slavery. They blasted the president in speech after speech throughout 1861 and 1862. When Lincoln finally issued the Emancipation Proclamation in late 1862, some Radicals objected because it did not free all the slaves. Still, when the vote came up in Congress for or against the proclamation, they voted in favor of it.

The Radicals also tried to gain control over the military, forming a committee called the Joint Committee on the Conduct of the War. This group used its power to investigate the war effort. The committee did some important work, such as exposing corruption in purchasing military supplies.

In some other ways, however, the committee was destructive. Its members wanted to use it to gain power over the army. They often targeted generals who were Democrats or who were suspected of not being sufficiently opposed to slavery. They never gained the power to remove anyone from command, but they did manage to ruin the careers of some officers by making clear their opposition to them.

The president and the Radicals in Congress also disagreed over how to treat the South. Lincoln was willing to make things relatively easy for the Southern states to return to the Union, while the Radicals wanted to punish the South. In 1864, the Radicals pushed through the Wade-Davis Bill, which set harsh terms for handling the South. Lincoln vetoed it, so the bill never became law. This disagreement was not resolved before Lincoln was killed in 1865.

Lincoln and the Dissenters

Some Democrats, called the "War Democrats," supported Lincoln's policies. The majority, however, opposed all or part of his plans and actions. Many of these Democrats fiercely criticized Lincoln, and most strongly opposed the emancipation policy. Some wanted to end the war immediately and negotiate a peace with the Confederates. They hoped that by offering to leave slavery alone, they

THADDEUS STEVENS

Born in Vermont in 1792, Thaddeus Stevens graduated from Dartmouth College. In 1815, he moved to Pennsylvania to practice law. He settled in the town of Gettysburg and became known as a champion of the poor. Deeply opposed to slavery, he often defended African Americans accused of being fugitive slaves without charging a fee.

Stevens served in the Pennsylvania state legislature in the 1830s and in the U.S. House of Representatives in the early 1850s. He joined the Republican party and was elected to the House once more in 1858, where he remained for the rest of his life. He played a major role in the presidency of Andrew Johnson, who followed Lincoln.

Stevens died in 1868. He was buried, as he had requested, in a cemetery that held blacks. In this way, his tombstone explained, he showed the principle he devoutly believed in— "Equality of man before his Creator."

This pro-Republican cartoon shows a determined "Union" fighting three "Copperheads." Democrats who wanted to end the war were nicknamed after the poisonous snake.

could persuade the Southern states to rejoin the Union. Others were willing to fight the war to restore the Union but agreed to do nothing to end slavery.

Democratic critics of the administration were called "Copperheads," after a poisonous American snake. Ohio's Clement Vallandigham, one of their leaders, toured the country giving speeches against the war. Eventually, he was seized by military officials, tried, and found guilty of expressing "sympathy" for the enemy and of speaking

A campaign flag for Abraham Lincoln and Andrew Johnson. Note that the stars in the blue field have been rearranged to spell the word *free*.

"disloyal sentiments." He was sentenced to prison for the duration of the war.

This action violated Vallandigham's rights. Lincoln knew it and had not wanted the trial, but he accepted the result to get Vallandigham out of the way. He changed the sentence to banishment to the South.

Vallandigham's case was not the only example of abuse of power. Early in the war, it was not clear whether Maryland would stay in the Union. If it joined the South, Confederate states would surround Washington, D.C. Lincoln moved quickly. He suspended habeas corpus in Maryland, allowing the government to hold people in prison without trial. Some of these prisoners were merely suspected of approving of the South seceding. Others had burned bridges and torn down telegraph wires, trying to disrupt communications between Washington, D.C., and the rest of the country. Ruling on an appeal of one of these cases, Chief Justice of the Supreme Court Robert Taney said that the action was unconstitutional. Lincoln simply ignored Taney's ruling, however. During 1862, the situation in Maryland calmed down, and Lincoln eventually ordered the release of these prisoners.

With these actions, Lincoln proved ready to extend his power in the effort to win the war. Still, his government never tried to suppress all opposition to its policies; attacks against Lincoln and his actions continued throughout the war.

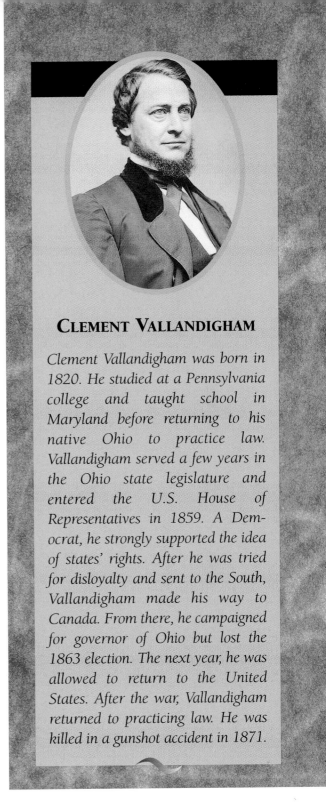

CLEMENT VALLANDIGHAM

Clement Vallandigham was born in 1820. He studied at a Pennsylvania college and taught school in Maryland before returning to his native Ohio to practice law. Vallandigham served a few years in the Ohio state legislature and entered the U.S. House of Representatives in 1859. A Democrat, he strongly supported the idea of states' rights. After he was tried for disloyalty and sent to the South, Vallandigham made his way to Canada. From there, he campaigned for governor of Ohio but lost the 1863 election. The next year, he was allowed to return to the United States. After the war, Vallandigham returned to practicing law. He was killed in a gunshot accident in 1871.

CHAPTER SEVEN

Telling the Story of the War

Newspapers were the main source of news from the front and also provided information to the soldiers fighting there. Here, a *New York Herald* wagon delivers newspapers to the troops at the front.

The War in Words

Newspapers from both sides sent as many as five hundred reporters along with the armies. Three were women, although these reporters were based in Washington, D.C. The educated son of a well-to-do Pennsylvania family, T. Morris Chester was the sole African-American reporter.

Commanders often cooperated with reporters; some officers apparently hoped to improve their own images by getting favorable coverage. Others thought little of the reporters. Union general William T. Sherman dismissed them for "their limited and tainted observations . . . [of] events they neither see nor comprehend."

President Lincoln apparently saw reporters more favorably and often invited them to talk to him about what they had seen with the armies.

One problem that plagued both sides was that newspapers could reveal vital information. Confederate generals learned about the movements of Union armies from the Northern papers. The reverse was also true. To prevent the enemy from learning where their troops were, some generals simply did not allow reporters to travel with their armies. Confederate general P. G. T. Beauregard asked Southern newspaper editors to delete any information from their stories that the North would find useful.

"[President Davis is] ready for any quarrel with any and everybody, at any time and all times; and the suspicion goes that rather than not have a row on hand with an enemy, he would make one with the best friend he had on earth."

Richmond Whig newspaper, 1864

Commenting on the War

During the 1860s, many newspapers made no effort to make their reports objective. Papers were often owned by politicians, who used their editorials to promote their views and also often slanted the news reports on events to support their positions. Thus, the North had pro-Lincoln papers, abolitionist papers that criticized the administration for not moving quickly enough to end slavery, Democratic papers that blasted the president for trying to force racial equality, and papers that took a range of other positions.

Many newspapers in the South were generous in their criticism of Confederate president Jefferson Davis's government. In 1862, the *Richmond Mercury* complained that Davis "treats all men as if they were idiotic insects."

The War in Pictures

Printing technology of the 1860s did not allow newspapers to print enough copies to meet daily demand or include photographs. Since the public wanted to see illustrations of the war, the solution was to hire an illustrator to sketch a picture. Workers back at the publisher's office carved wood blocks following the patterns on the sketch to use for printing.

Frank Leslie's Illustrated Newspaper and *Harper's Weekly* both added prints to their stories about the war. These papers displayed the

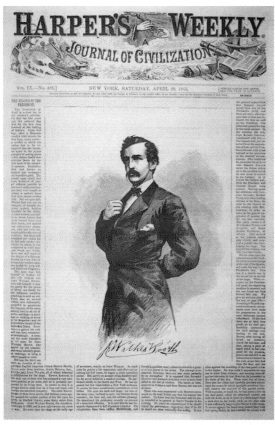

work of very skilled artists. Winslow Homer—later a famous U.S. painter—made drawings for *Harper's*, as did Alfred Waud. Edwin Forbes was a talented illustrator for *Leslie's*.

The South was cut off from these illustrated papers. One publisher created the *Southern Illustrated News*, which ran from 1862 to 1865, to fill the gap.

Left: On April 29, 1865, *Harper's Weekly* included an illustration of John Wilkes Booth, Lincoln's assassin.

Below: One person who saw Matthew Brady's pictures of Antietam wrote, "Mr. Brady has brought home the terrible earnestness of war. If he has not brought bodies and laid them in our dooryards, he has done something very like it."

While photographs of the war were not published in newspapers, photographs were taken. Photographers could not take action shots because cameras of the day needed to expose the film for ten seconds to produce a picture. Dedicated to recording the war, they roamed army camps and battlefields to take thousands of pictures.

The mastermind behind many of these photographs was Mathew Brady, who hired a team of twenty photographers to document the war. Some of these photographers were highly skilled and resented the fact that Brady never allowed the actual photographers to gain any credit. Some quit in anger.

In October 1862, Brady displayed photos taken after the bloody Battle of Antietam, in Maryland, the month before. Among them were images of dead soldiers, their bodies lying in contorted positions. These pictures shocked the viewing public.

Brady's images, news reports, and the letters of soldiers made it clear that the war was not the glorious business that many had expected back in 1861. Despite the horrors of war and the deep personal losses that tens of thousands of families suffered, people on both sides continued to support the war effort because they strongly believed in the causes they were fighting for.

MATHEW BRADY

Mathew Brady was born in rural New York in 1823 and opened a photography studio in New York City in 1844. Brady took pictures of every well-known American of his time, becoming famous for these pictures, which were collected in an 1850 book.

When the Civil War broke out, Brady was determined to document it in pictures. He took only a few of them himself, leaving the work to his hired hands.

Brady's great effort destroyed him financially. He had borrowed heavily to fund the program, believing that the government would buy his pictures. It didn't. A nationwide financial crisis in 1873 worsened his situation, and he had to sell his studio. He did not even have the money to store his negatives, which the War Department bought for very little money. Two years later, Congress granted Brady $25,000, but it was not enough to restore his fortune. He died in 1896 in the charity ward of a hospital.

1861 *Feb. 8:* Confederate states adopt their new Constitution.
Feb. 18: Jefferson Davis inaugurated as president of the Confederacy.
Apr. 12: South fires on Fort Sumter in South Carolina, beginning the war.
May 20: Confederate Congress moves capital to Richmond, Virginia.
Aug. 5: U.S. Congress passes country's first income tax law.
Oct. 24: Voters in western Virginia approve creation of separate state.
Dec. 10: U.S. Congress forms Joint Committee on the Conduct of the War.

1862 *Feb. 25:* U.S. Congress allows government to print "greenbacks," paper money not backed by gold.
Feb. 27: Confederate Congress gives Davis power to suspend habeas corpus.
Apr. 16: U.S. Congress ends slavery in District of Columbia.
May 20: U.S. Congress passes Homestead Act, opening public land for settlement.
June 19: U.S. Congress frees slaves in territories.
July 1: U.S. Congress passes far-reaching tax law; Lincoln signs the Pacific Railroad Act.
July 2: U.S. Congress passes Morrill Act.
July 17: U.S. Congress gives freedom to Southern slaves who escape to the Union army.
Oct. 17: Confederate draft law exempts men owning twenty or more slaves.

1863 *Jan. 1:* Lincoln issues Emancipation Proclamation.
Apr. 2: Mob in Richmond riots, looting stores.
Apr. 24: Confederate Congress passes major tax act.
May 6: Clement Vallandigham tried for disloyalty.
June 20: West Virginia officially becomes a state.
July 12–17: Draft riots occur in New York City.
Oct. 3: Lincoln proclaims Thanksgiving as a national holiday.

1864 *Oct. 31:* Nevada becomes a state.

1865 *Feb. 3:* Peace conference at Hampton Roads, Virginia, fails to settle conflict.
Mar. 3: U.S. Congress creates Freedmen's Bureau.
Apr. 2: Confederate government leaves Richmond.
May 10: President Davis captured by Union forces.
June 19: Union forces announce the end of slavery in Texas.

Glossary

antipathy: a strong feeling of dislike.

blockade: to prevent enemy ships from carrying goods into or out of ports during a war.

bonds: loans in which an investor pays the government a certain amount of money and receives the promise that the government will repay that money, plus interest, at a later date.

Border States: the states on the northern edge of the southern states, where there was slavery, but it was not a very strong part of society; includes Delaware, Maryland, Kentucky, and Missouri.

casualties: the men killed, wounded, captured, and missing in a battle.

civil rights: the rights belonging to individuals because they are citizens of a nation.

Confederacy: also called "the South;" another name for the Confederate States of America, the nation formed by the states that had seceded—Virginia, Tennessee, North Carolina, South Carolina, Georgia, Alabama, Mississippi, Louisiana, Texas, Arkansas, and Florida.

constitution: the basic laws and principles of a nation that outline the powers of the government and the rights of the people.

demoralized: weakened in confidence.

draft: a law that requires men of a certain age to join the army.

exemption: a rule freeing a person from a duty or obligation.

habeas corpus: the rule that forces a government holding someone under arrest to charge that person with a crime and hold a trial.

martial law: rule by the military, during which normal laws are set aside.

secede: to leave the Union.

segregation: the policy of having separate facilities for blacks and whites.

sovereign: self-governing, independent.

strike: stopping work to get better pay, hours, or working conditions.

textile mills: factories that make cloth from cotton or wool.

Union: also called "the North;" another name for the United States of America, which, after secession, included Maine, New Hampshire, Vermont, Massachusetts, Rhode Island, Connecticut, New York, New Jersey, Pennsylvania, Delaware, Maryland, Ohio, Michigan, Indiana, Illinois, Kentucky, Wisconsin, Minnesota, Iowa, Kansas, Missouri, Oregon, and California; in 1863, West Virginia seceded from Virginia and entered the Union as a separate state.

Further Resources

These books and web sites cover the life of civilians during the Civil War and the actions of the Union and Confederate governments:

WEB SITES

www.civilwarhome.com Follow links on this Civil War enthusiast's homepage to essays on the Civil War, biographies, and letters to and from soldiers.

www.civil-war.net The Civil War Home Page web site includes selected documents by Lincoln and others, including entries of soldiers' diaries and letters home, a detailed time line, and images of war.

www.homepages.dsu.edu/jankej/civil-war/civilwar.htm An index web site lists numerous articles on a wide range of Civil War topics, including home life, news–papers, and women in the Civil War. Also includes way to search for individual Civil War soldiers and sailors.

sunsite.utk.edu/civil-war/warweb.html The American Civil War web site contains a number of links to resources, including images of wartime, Civil War re-enactors, and biographical information.

BOOKS

Arnold, James R. *Life Goes On: The Civil War at Home, 1861–1865*. Minneapolis, MN: Lerner Publications, 2002.

Beller, Susan Provost. *Confederate Ladies of Richmond*. Brookfield, CT: Twenty-First Century Books, 1999.

Biel, Timothy Levi. *Life in the North during the Civil War* (The Way People Live). San Diego, CA: Lucent Books, 1997.

Bolotin, Norman. *The Civil War A to Z: A Young Readers' Guide to over 100 People, Places, and Points of Importance*. New York: Dutton, 2002.

Brooks, Victor. *African Americans in the Civil War* (Untold History of the Civil War). Philadelphia, PA: Chelsea House Publishers, 2000.

Clinton, Catherine. *Scholastic Encyclopedia of the Civil War*. New York: Scholastic Books, 1999.

Currie, Stephen. *Women of the Civil War* (Women in History). San Diego, CA: Lucent Books, 2002.

Damon, Duane. *Growing Up in the Civil War, 1861 to 1865*. Minneapolis, MN: Lerner Publications, 2003.

Editors of Time-Life. *The Time-Life History of the Civil War*. New York: Barnes and Noble Books, 1995.

Smith, Carter, ed. *Behind the Lines: A Sourcebook on the Civil War* (American Albums from the Collections of the Library of Congress). Brookfield, CT: Millbrook Press, 1993.

Sullivan, George. *Portraits of War: Civil War Photographers and Their Work*. Brookfield, CT: Twenty-First Century Books, 1998.

Index

Page numbers in *italics* indicate maps and diagrams.